TWELVE WHO WERE CHOSEN

THE DISCIPLES OF JESUS

TWELVE WHO WERE CHOSEN

THE DISCIPLES OF JESUS

WILLIAM P. BARKER

BARBOUR BOOKS
Westwood, New Jersey

Printed in the United States of America
ISBN 1-55748-185-7

Published by Barbour and Company, Inc.
P.O. Box 1219
Westwood, New Jersey

TO

MY MOTHER AND FATHER

Contents

ANDREW

1

Andrew

MOST OF US have at least two mistaken ideas about the Twelve Apostles.

Mistaken idea number one is that the Twelve Apostles were a group of unusually gifted, exceptionally talented, deeply religious and naturally saintly men.

Mistaken idea number two is that one must do something big and dramatic to be a Christian.

The Apostle Andrew shows how mistaken are both these ideas. Andrew never preached like Peter or wrote like Matthew. He never traveled like Paul, or held office like James. He was not a creative thinker like John.

Andrew was only an ordinary businessman who ran a small fishing outfit on Galilee. He never made any headlines. In fact, Andrew is only mentioned fourteen times in the Bible.

Nevertheless, Jesus chose him to be one of The Twelve and his name is carried on every roster of apostles in the New Testament. Interestingly enough, Andrew's name is always among the first four names in every list of apostles.

There is something likeable about Andrew. He was plain, practical, modest and to-the-point. He was a man of decision. After he spent an afternoon, an evening and part of the night talking with Jesus, he made up his mind, resolving to go all-out for Jesus. He was Christ's man through and through.

Andrew was a man of courage. He was the first disciple. It always takes courage to be first in anything.

Andrew was a man of thought. He was quiet, but deep-thinking. He was a man on a search and his words at the end of his search, though simple and to-the-point, reveal a man who had done a lot of thinking: "We have found the Messiah."

Andrew was a man of action. He never had much to say; he believed in doing. Whenever he is mentioned in the New Testament, he is bringing someone to meet Jesus. Andrew was not busy just being busy, as are so many church people. He was the right kind of activist. He was busy introducing people to Jesus. By sharing Jesus, he knew he could keep what Jesus had done for him. Unlike so many of us, Andrew was a conductor instead of a receiver and he answers the question: What can an ordinary person do?

Andrew made no dramatic decision to dash off to the foreign missionary field. He didn't insist on getting a crowd to listen to him. Like most of us, Andrew went through life without doing anything particularly dramatic. Yet, Andrew was indispensable.

Andrew took the Christian message to single individuals, and one of the first he contacted was his brother, Simon. Without Andrew, there might not have been a Simon Peter in history, and think how much poorer Christian history would be without Peter!

It is often harder to interest relatives in Christ than it is to interest a stranger. Any minister can tell about the number of times people call upon him to interest a member of their family in Christianity. Almost invariably, the person making the contact adds, "But don't let on to so-and-so that I called you." To which anyone should reply, "And why not?"

Andrew knew that in his own family he could be more effective than anyone else. The mass-evangelism campaigns have their place with the packed halls, jammed stadiums, massed choirs and droves of decisions, but they often lack the personal touch. God still uses individuals to reach other individuals. God uses individuals like Andrew, and us, to reach the hard-to-gets.

We could call Andrew the first home missionary. Any newspaper will reveal the need for home missionaries in twentieth-century American homes, yet we think Christianity has to be big and dramatic. The biggest, most dramatic work anyone can do is to let Jesus be alive in a home.

Andrew was a humble man. He could do his work, then fade quietly from the scene. He must have known he would be overshadowed by Simon Peter, who was obviously the more able of the two brothers. It wasn't long until Andrew was being referred to and identified as "Simon Peter's brother."

It is never pleasant to be overshadowed by a younger brother and Andrew had to go through life as the unknown relative of a great man. A lesser man than Andrew could have resented being eclipsed by Simon Peter and might have stooped to jealousy, but Andrew was big enough to let his brother appear the bigger. In many ways, it was Andrew who was the bigger of the two, for he had a humility which forgot about self. He did his work without seeking applause. He didn't care who got the limelight because he put Christ first.

Andrew was the key man on several occasions. On the day the five thousand were fed, it was Andrew who found the boy with the lunch of loaves and fishes. Andrew saw possibilities. Others might have seen only a restless youngster and might have scolded the boy and sent him back to the crowd, but Andrew used the resources of the boy.

We often forget that we were once restless, energetic and mischievous youngsters. So were Dwight Eisenhower, Albert Schweitzer and Martin Luther. And so were Al Capone and Adolf Hitler and Karl Marx. Andrew saw a child, and he saw opportunity. It would be interesting to learn what became of that boy with the loaves and fishes. At least we can be sure that the boy was introduced to Jesus by a man who knew the possibilities in both Jesus and little boys.

Someone once asked why it is that charming and interesting little boys can grow up to be such disagreeable old men. One answer: there aren't enough of us who will be Andrews.

Andrew was the perfect church usher, ready to welcome anyone to Jesus. One day, a group of strangers lingered near Jesus. They were Greek-speaking Jews or outsiders who had approached the Apostle Philip about being introduced to Jesus. Philip, however, was a bit cautious. He didn't know whether Jesus should bother with strangers. Philip might even have had all the arguments we hear today: there's enough work to do here among our own people; you can't trust these "foreigners"; they might be subversive.

Andrew knew God is no respecter of persons. He met the Greeks, welcomed them and saw to it that they met

Jesus. In a sense, Andrew was also the first foreign missionary.

Andrew's act took courage. It is not easy to stand up for Jesus—or to stand up for strangers. We need some Andrews who remember that outsiders are people, too. Because they are human beings, they are God's people. To God, the color of a man's skin, or the place of his birth, or the sound of his name, or the accent of his speech mean absolutely nothing. Andrew was enough of a man to put this faith into action.

Andrew's name in Greek means "brave" or "manly." He lived the name to the hilt and tradition claims he even died that way. When he finished his work at Patrae in Achaia, the reports state that he was tied, not nailed, to a cross in the shape of an X, to prolong his agony as much as possible. Thus passed on an ordinary, garden-variety man who was a believer in and a doer for Jesus Christ. An ordinary, garden-variety man—that's you or I!

Yet the ordinary, garden-variety person has tremendous capacities for discipleship. Get to know Jesus; then find others. In God's economy, this is big business!

SIMON PETER

2

Simon Peter

HE WAS A young sailor. He had spent so much of his life on the water that he seemed to have taken on some of the sea's characteristics. Like the sea, he had a violent temper and quickly changing moods.

Like most sailors, he knew how to use his hands—for violence, if necessary. He had a hasty tongue, and was known as an impetuous, unstable young man.

Yet, for all that, people liked him. He was seldom anywhere long before people knew of his presence. He had color. There was something dashing, even debonair, about him that people couldn't help but notice and like, despite his recklessness. He was a typical kid brother, a marked contrast to his sober, steady brother, Andrew. His name was Simon.

It was his older brother Andrew who brought him to meet Jesus. Perhaps Andrew thought it would be good for Simon to meet Jesus. Perhaps it would give him some religion. It seems more likely, however, that the two brothers had often talked together on deeper things in life. It also seems likely that Andrew and Simon had talked together about a Messiah.

A Messiah was badly needed. Most Jews hoped that the God-sent Anointed One would come soon and deliver them from their oppressors. The Jews were sick of taxes and the burdens of Rome's tyranny. They had tired of the harsh legalism of their religious leaders.

Andrew and Simon, like thousands of other Jews, were looking for a Messiah. Andrew was the first to meet Jesus, and after a long talk with Him, Andrew was convinced. Jesus was the man.

Curiosity probably brought younger brother Simon to meet Jesus. Who was this carpenter of Nazareth who had so impressed older brother Andrew? It wasn't quite like Andrew to be so carried away by anything. Simon was interested.

Jesus opened the interview. "So you are Simon." Apparently He'd heard of Simon from Andrew. Seeming to size him up, Jesus spoke again, and those nearby who knew Simon must have collapsed with laughter. Jesus told Simon, "From now on, your name shall be 'Peter.' "

The joke was this: "Peter" is the word for "rock."

(Our words "petroleum" and "petrified" come from the same root.) It was as though Jesus had called shifting-sand Simon the nickname, "Old Gibraltar." Everyone who knew Simon realized the contradiction of the name to the man's character, and it was a wonderful joke on Simon. The name "Peter" (or "Rock") got the same laugh as the name "Tiny" when applied to a six-foot, two-hundred pound giant, or "Curley" when calling a bald man. "Peter" was exactly opposite of Simon.

The name stuck and was always good for a laugh. It was far different, however, where Jesus was concerned. Others saw only weaknesses in Simon and Jesus saw these, too. But Jesus saw other qualities as well. He saw potentialities in Simon that no one else had seen, and offered the nickname "Peter" as a challenge. It spoke of His faith and hope in Simon. The name "Peter" challenged Simon to live up to His faith and hope. It put backbone into his life and Simon rose from being a moral amoeba to a moral vertebrate.

That is the way Jesus acts. He offers to every man a challenge to live a new life. Many men have tried to live *down* nicknames, but Simon tried to live *up to* his nickname. With impetuosity that was typical of Simon Peter, he decided on the spot that he would follow Jesus.

He had many slips, and there were many occasions when he was anything but the rock his nickname implied. He was self-centered. When Jesus said that following Him meant sacrifice, Simon interrupted with assurance born of conceit, "We have forsaken all . . . what shall we have therefore?" In other words, "What's in it for me? What do I get out of it?"

Simon was rash. One night, he and others were in a boat on Galilee when they saw Jesus. Simon impetuously jumped overboard and made for Jesus, but he panicked and nearly drowned. Fortunately, Jesus grabbed him in time.

Simon was shallow. He did not agree that Jesus had to die. He argued that you could love, yet avoid sacrifice and would not listen to Jesus' ideas on the subject. When he tried to talk Jesus out of the Cross, he made such a nuisance of himself that Jesus took him to task. Sharply, Jesus told Simon that he was hindering God's work, and ordered him to stop his devilish claptrap: "Get thee behind me Satan!"

Mercurial Simon was a talker. Promises came easy, too easy, and some think he was fickle. Probably it was a case of the hot-and-cold allegiance that most of us give to Jesus. In any case, it was easy for Simon to promise in stirring words at the Last Supper, "Though they all fall away because of you, I will never fall away" (R.S.V.). It was just as easy for the same man who had just spoken these nobly sounding phrases to be laughed out of his faith by a servant girl. Big-talking Simon disgraced himself. When the chips were down a few hours after Jesus' arrest, Simon denied vigorously that (1) he was a companion of Jesus; (2) he even knew Jesus; (3) he had anything whatsoever to do with Jesus. Simon was hardly a rock!

Yet, the man who was like shifting sand little by little became Peter the Rock, and we could call Simon's story, "The Transfiguration of the Unlikely." He eventually became a man who lived up to his nickname.

On the road to Caesarea-Philippi, there is a spring where most travelers stopped. Over the spring is carved an inscription to Baal which Jesus and the others probably saw. Perhaps it inspired Jesus to ask His disciples, "But whom say ye that I am?"

Various ones gave hesitant, tentative answers. Then Simon had a flash of vision that the others lacked. He startled everyone with the conviction, "Thou art the Christ, the son of the living God!" The words were like a bugle! They raised curtains and opened windows in the minds of the others. Simon had a moment of penetrating insight that comes occasionally to every man.

Jesus, in effect, said to Simon, "You *are* Peter, the Rock. You are impetuous, vacillating, denying, courageous and witnessing—typical of all men. All these things are wrapped up in human personality. Yet, realizing your weakness and your strength—for I have no other way than the witness of frail men—on you and on men like you I must and I shall build my church."

When we confess that Jesus is the Christ, God ventures to build His church on us. He depends upon every believer to keep the faith alive and growing, to insure the coming of Christ's kingdom on earth.

Jesus was crucified and laid away in a tomb. He was quite dead, and the authorities dusted off their hands with the certainty that things would soon get back to normal. But things have never been normal since then. Three days later, people claimed that Jesus was very much alive again. They asserted that God had raised Him from the dead.

We are inclined to take a coldly skeptical attitude toward this news. When a man is dead, he is dead. We know. A report of Jesus' being raised from the dead is hard to believe, and we debate whether or not it is possible. We debate what happened. We demand some sort of "proof."

The best "proof" lies in the lives of the people who believed in the resurrection and who lived by it. There can be no doubt that something happened to them.

Simon Peter is one of the best examples. After the resurrection and the coming of the Holy Spirit, Simon really became a rock. He knew that he was exposing himself to arrest, punishment and possibly death. He knew that he was exposing himself to ridicule. But he fearlessly sought a good public place where a crowd could gather, and he started to preach. His preaching rocked

Jerusalem, and won thousands as believers in the good news of Jesus Christ.

The same Simon who had been laughed out of his faith by a little servant girl was not afraid to stand up to the highest officials of the state and church. Although threatened with torture and ordered to keep quiet, the new Simon could not be cowed. "We ought to obey God rather than men," he stoutly answered.

All this time, the name Peter had stuck. Formerly a joke, it now became a compliment. Simon was Peter, the Rock; he was immovable. The stability and strength about the man made him a steadfast leader in the Christian church until the end of his life and tradition is strong that he died a martyr at Rome.

Simon Peter is an example of the possibilities that Jesus sees in every man or woman. At present, most of us are people who can see only our problems. But there is a "Thou shalt be" in each of us because Jesus sees our possibilities. By the power of Christ, those possibilities can be translated into realities.

There is a tame, dull, grey respectability that often passes for the Christian life. If you think it is Christianity, you are mistaken. Jesus did not come to call you to that kind of living. Too many Christian churches are religious museums housing a lot of pious mummies, but Christ calls out to people like Peter and you, with all your weaknesses and limitations. He sees your potentialities and possibilities!

Jesus sees possibilities in you that are seen by no one else, not even you. He can size you up for your real self and give you a glimpse of your real destiny. You find your true personality only with Christ and you receive the assurance of new character as soon as you meet Him. To you, He gives the promise of a job to do. He assigns you a place in the kingdom. You are *useful.*

There is an angel in every block of marble, but no matter how rough-hewn, a master sculptor can bring it out. There is a disciple, a man or woman of God, standing in every human life. No matter how chipped or rough-hewn, the Master-carpenter can carve it out.

Thou art————————(put your name here). Thou shalt be a rock!

JAMES, SON OF ZEBEDEE

3

James, Son of Zebedee

THE DISCIPLES DID not have halos; neither did they strike pious poses or wear twenty yards of silk to work. (Anyone can see they would have tripped and got tangled up in such a get-up!) Nor did the disciples have the sweet expressions, beatific smiles and upturned eyes that artists have given them.

Take any of Jesus' disciples out of the stained glass windows and see how human they really were. They were amazingly similar in temperament and make-up to so many of us!

James, for instance, was economically a bit better off than the average. He and a brother and father owned a fishing boat on Galilee and had men working for them.

Like many of us, James was a comparatively young man when he began to follow Christ. Like many of us, he was rather ordinary. There was nothing dashing or dramatic in James as there was in Peter. Good old plain James was not the type who would be elected president of his class. He was more like the fellow third from the end, second row, in the class picture, whose name you wish you could remember ten years later.

Peter could dramatically exclaim, "Even if I must die with you, I will not deny you . . . Though they all fall away . . . I will never . . ." (R.S.V.).

Thomas could say with a flourish, "Let us also go, that we may die with him."

Not James. He simply had no flair for the dramatic. Yet Jesus chose him as one of The Twelve. There were a lot of disciples among the hundreds of people who followed Jesus, but Jesus picked James to be one of the special group for special jobs.

Apparently, James was even held in special esteem by Jesus, since James' name is always either second or third in the list of disciples. Time and time again, James' name pops up as one of three who were apparently special in Jesus' eyes: "*Peter, James* and *John.*" Who was present at the healing of Peter's mother-in-law? Peter, James and John. Who was on hand at the raising of Jairus' daughter? Peter, James and John. Who witnessed the transfiguration? Peter, James and John, again. And so on, time after time, Peter, James and John—the inner circle.

The lessons for us are obvious. We don't have to be dashing, dramatic personalities to be useful to Christ. A plain, sincere person is as welcome and as necessary as anyone. Neither must we be great talkers or speakers to be useful to Christ.

James had his share of human frailties, and two incidents in the gospels are not at all to his credit. One occurred on the day Jesus and The Twelve were going up to Jerusalem for the Passover. To get from Galilee to Jerusalem, they had to pass through Samaria, and Samaritans and Jews mixed like oil and water. Nevertheless, when it was getting dark, Jesus sent a couple of disciples into a Samaritan village to arrange for spending the night. The villagers behaved contemptibly. Maybe it was the disciples' fault, maybe the Samaritans'; probably both were at fault. In any case, Jesus was not allowed to stay overnight in the village because He and His friends were Jews.

James blew up. That narrow-minded, hate-filled hick town! Refusing to let Jesus stay overnight! This was too much for James. Such inhuman, vindictive people did not deserve to live. James turned to Jesus and ordered Him to send fire down upon the village.

"Send down fire!" It was an angry man who spat those

words, but God never takes orders from anyone. God never sends down fire to punish people into line.

Jesus saw how cruel and petty the Samaritans were, and He knew that James' desire of cruelty for cruelty was not the answer. Jesus realized He had been insulted, but trading insult for insult would have accomplished nothing. He came not to destroy the world but to save it; He came that they might have life and have it more abundantly.

James had a temper. James got mad. Probably that is why Jesus nicknamed James and his brother John "Sons of Thunder."

James got angry at the wrong things. How like us, fretting about people instead of causes, angry about little things instead of big things. It is all right to get angry about the right things, and Jesus likes men and women with a temper—people of passion. He would like us to get angry at times, angry about conditions existing among underprivileged people, for example.

James was gradually able to channel his temper and discipline himself so that passion was guided in the right directions. Fire from Heaven fell on James: the fire of the Holy Spirit which transformed him into an effective man of passion for Christ.

James and his brother John had known Jesus well—better than the rest, perhaps. They believed in Him. Somehow, they began to think they would like the highest ranks and noblest titles in this kingdom Jesus described. Maybe they were a bit jealous of Peter and wanted to make sure he would not out-rank them.

Ambitious James, with the wrong kind of ambition. Jesus likes ambitious people—people with the *right kind of ambition.* He wants men who have the ambition to be fellow workers and fellow sufferers with Him. He wants men and women who have the ambition to attempt great things for God and who expect great things from God.

Through his friendship with and devotion to Jesus, James was changed. His ambition was molded to the kind of drive that can change lives, make a Christian home and better a community.

By nature, James was like most of us—angry over wrong things and ambitious in the wrong ways. By God's help he was changed so that these traits could be used by God. You, too, can be changed so that your anger and ambition will serve Him.

Ten or twelve years after the crucifixion, King Herod was looking for a way to increase his popularity. To please many of his subjects, he decided to stamp out the obnoxious heresy known as the Christian church. He wanted to execute the most prominent Christian leader in the Jerusalem church. Who was it? The man with the most passion for the Christ, the most ambitions for the church—James, of course. And so, in 44 A.D., James was chopped in half by Herod's executioner. He was the first of The Twelve to die for his faith.

He must have been a comparatively young man—perhaps still in his thirties, although probably in his forties. But it is not how *long* we live; it is how *much* we live. It is better to lose your life for Christ's sake than to save it for your own sake.

Discipleship *costs*. There is a Cross in Christianity which costs time, possessions, pride and sometimes even life itself!

The story of James' death in the Book of Acts is brief, taking up only two lines. The story then goes on to relate how Peter was thrown into jail by Herod during the same period of persecution. There are no embellishments on the story of James. Two lines; no more.

For every one who receives the Congressional Medal of Honor, there are equally as many, just as brave, who did not get one. Men may forget their names, but no name is ever forgotten by God.

The church is full of Jameses. Most of us are plain people who have a knack for getting angry and have a tendency toward ambition. But Christ needs us. Put those same qualities at His disposal and see what He can do with them. The church and the world depend upon plain folks with the *right* kind of anger and the *right* kind of ambition.

JOHN

4

John

More men are named John than any other name. More baby boys are christened John than any other name. Maybe it is due to family tradition, or because the name means "God is gracious" in Hebrew. Maybe it is because John is the name of "the disciple whom Jesus loved."

Artists misrepresent John. Usually they depict him as a delicate, beardless dreamer. Some even have John looking effeminate. Even the New Testament phrase that John was "the disciple Jesus loved" implies he was a lovable person. Far from it!

There was something powerful, startling and electric about John. He was a child of storm. Like his native Sea of Galilee, on which he made his living by fishing, he was given to hot, terrible outbursts, tornadoes of anger and whirlwinds of enthusiasm; so much so, that Jesus nicknamed him, Son of Thunder.

Not only was he a hot-head, but occasionally other parts of the New Testament reveal him to be an all-too-human figure; for example, the time John saw a man using Jesus' name to cast out demons. The man was not one of the disciple band, but was helping mentally ill people in the name of Jesus. John was intolerant and self-righteous. He loudly and insistently ordered the healer to stop. Then, he conceitedly reported to Jesus what he had done. Obviously, John expected to be commended, but Jesus had no patience for men with a misguided sense of self-importance. Furthermore, He was happy to see anyone using His name to help others.

John was narrow-minded. Because someone did not belong to his group or party, John thought he was automatically wrong. Thus, we gather a picture of John as a conceited hot-head—the picture of a man as human as any of us.

Yet, Jesus chose John to be a disciple, and even took him into the inner circle, for John's name is always one of the first three mentioned. The fact that Jesus called John is an indication that Jesus has work for *you* and *me*.

It is a commentary also that Jesus can change human

personality, for He certainly changed John. What transformed John from a conceited Son of Thunder to a Child of God was association with Jesus. But what was it about Jesus that most affected John?

Perhaps it was the Last Supper. The disciples were a tense, jealous group, and John had squabbled with the others over who had done the most, who was the most important, and who deserved the greatest reward. Jesus, walking in at the height of this childishness, said nothing. He quietly filled a basin, walked to the first man, and did an astounding thing. He performed slave's work —the menial, unpleasant job of washing the disciples' feet. No one wanted to serve in this capacity; it was beneath their dignity. Regardless of the relief and comfort it brought to others, they all thought it degrading and humiliating to wash feet.

The foot-washing episode was illustrative of words spoken later that evening: "A new commandment I give unto you, That ye love one another . . . By this shall all men know that ye are my disciples." We shall see how those words remained with John the rest of his life. He never forgot them. John was cleansed of more than dust and sweat on his feet and ankles. He was cleansed of pride.

Was it the crucifixion that most deeply affected John? The Friend of the conceited, the One who understood even tough-headed Sons of Thunder, was willing to die for *them?* Did John suddenly feel, "He cares enough for a self-righteous hot-head like me to die for me! He really means it when He says God loves us!"?

Was it Jesus' words to him shortly before His death when He entrusted Mary, His mother, to John? Did John suddenly see that Jesus believed in him, trusted in him and expected much of him?

Probably it was a combination of all these events that changed John. In any case, we know he became one of the most effective Christian men who ever lived.

After the resurrection of Jesus, John was looked to as one of the leaders in the infant Christian church. As the movement spread north to Samaria, the parent church at Jerusalem thought it would be helpful to send a couple of experienced, mature believers to meet with the new converts, and John was one of the two picked for this important mission. John no longer thought only of John; he thought mostly of Jesus. At Samaria, he humbly prayed for the new believers and quietly placed his hand on their heads, imparting the Holy Spirit to them. John was looked to as a channel of God's power.

People saw John as a man who had learned to discipline his terrible emotions and to channel his restless drive. Instead of being a Roman candle, he became a steadily burning torch.

John has been called the Christian Plato, and it is his writings that most impress us. There is no doubt that he had one of the most creative minds the world has ever known. He wrote the most deeply devotional treatise on Jesus we have ever known—the Gospel according to John. We could easily subtitle it, "What Jesus Means to Me."

To this book, we turn for consolation, and read the familiar words in the fourteenth chapter, "In my Father's house are many mansions. . . ." In John's gospel we find the idea that Jesus was actually with God from the very beginning; in fact, He is the pre-existent word of God. It was John who wrote what has been described as the gospel-in-a-nutshell: "For God so loved the world, that he gave his only begotten Son, that whosoever believeth in him should not perish, but have everlasting life." No one can really improve on that as a concise summary of Christianity.

Many scholars claim that this same John was the author of other parts of our New Testament. There are four other books of the twenty-seven New Testament books beside the Gospel of John that bear the name of John as author. These are the three letters of John, called I John, II John and III John; and the Revelation of John, the last book in the Bible. Some critics have wondered how one man could possibly write so much and over so long a period of time. Others have pointed out the similarities through all the New Testament writings bearing the name of John as author. One John or several Johns, there is one thread that runs through all the John-literature. This thread is the love of Jesus Christ.

Love seems to be the favorite word of John. He seems possessed by it. "For God so loved . . ." (John 3:16); "Beloved, let us love one another: for love is of God; and every one that loveth is born of God, and knoweth God. He that loveth not knoweth not God; for God is love . . ." (I John 4:7–8). Quite a change from the conceited "Son of Thunder."

John lived to extreme old age. Tradition agrees that he spent his later years in southwest Turkey, in Ephesus. In his declining years, when he was too weak to walk, he was carried to church. At the close of the service, he was often asked to say a few words, and invariably he whispered, "Little children, love one another."

One day, the story goes, someone asked him why he said these same words and nothing more. The old man answered, "Because this is our Lord's commandment and if we all fulfill this, nothing more is needed. For love is the fulfilling of the law." John could teach us how to grow old gracefully.

Something which demands more of our attention is the matter of old age. Statistics show we can expect to live much longer than either our fathers or grandfathers. In 1900, the life expectancy averaged only forty-seven years. Today it is around 68.4. Furthermore, if you hit sixty-five, you have a good chance to live another 13.6 years.

Medicine has done its part in keeping us alive, all right. But keeping us alive for what? We are reminded of the story of little Timmy who was told to help grandmother with bundles—"We want to save grandma." Let her have his room nearest the bathroom—"We want to save grandma the steps." The youngster finally burst out, "Mother, just what are we saving grandma for?"

Good question! For what will they keep you alive? To be a crotchety, self-centered *old* whiner, instead of a crotchety, self-centered *young* whiner?

Most of us think of retirement years only in terms of preparing for sixty-five, financially. That, of course, is important. But that is where most of us stop. It is far more important to prepare mentally, emotionally and spiritually.

Dr. Harold Hall of Harvard made a study of retirements. He found that those who failed in retirement had not prepared for what they would do with their time. Few failed because of inadequate financial preparation. In other words, medical science is keeping you alive, and social security and pension are keeping you going—for what? To keep on being a hot-headed, conceited Son of Thunder? Heaven forbid!

John in his old age wrote a series of three short letters. The first begins by talking about Jesus. "That which we have seen and heard declare we unto you. . . ." That is life, for a man of twenty or a man of eighty.

Get to know Christ. Hear Him. See Him wherever there is a human being in need. Let that love that was in Him transform you. Proclaim it in your acts and words to the members of your family, your business associates, your neighbors. Start now to be the person you want to be at sixty-five—and the person Christ wants you to be *now*.

PHILIP

5

Philip

JESUS CHOSE TWELVE men to be his closest friends and helpers. We call these men the Twelve Apostles, or the Disciples. Somehow, over the past 1900 years we have turned them into supermen, and we have clothed them with so much pious respect that we lose sight of them as human beings.

They were amazingly similar to us. Pick them out of the first century and drop them into the twentieth, and they would be so like us we could accept them as contemporaries. Take them out of Galilee, put them on Main Street, and they would belong.

Take the disciple Philip, for example.

Philip was a country boy from northern Galilee. He

lived in Bethsaida, which, translated, means "house of fish." In other words, Philip was from the fisherman's quarter or fishing town. Most scholars agree that Bethsaida was a section of Capernaum.

Philip fished for a living. One day a man approached and invited him to fish for more important catches—men. Philip became a charter member of the world's most famous fishing club, an exclusive fellowship which is open to anyone who accepts Jesus Christ's invitation. It is the oldest fishing club in the world, and one in which every one of us belongs.

Like so many of us, Philip never made the headlines; he was never a dashing, colorful figure. He was a practical man who could grasp a problem quickly and come up with an answer.

Take the time Jesus was preaching to a crowd on a remote hillside. As the time drew near midafternoon, Jesus was concerned about the crowd. He knew they were tired and faint from a long trip, and extreme hunger did not add to their comfort.

Jesus turned to Philip with the problem of feeding this large crowd. Philip, the practical man, did a bit of quick figuring. He might be an engineer or an accountant were he living today. With his tidy mind, he could do sums in his head. He studied the problem and came up with practical answers.

Assuming they could get enough bread easily and

quickly—a poor assumption since they were quite a distance from the nearest village—it would take at least 200 pennyworth, or forty dollars' worth to give a little to everyone. This was probably out of the question because they probably did not have that much money.

Practical Philip saw the need, all right, but there was nothing anyone could do. Oh, it was true that a little boy had come up with a few loaves and fishes, but that was insignificant. What help could they get from one boy's lunch?

Philip, for all his careful calculations, reckoned without Jesus Christ. He assumed, because his resources were insufficient, that he couldn't do the job.

One of our favorite stories is about the little English cobbler who became the first great modern foreign missionary. His name was William Carey. His favorite motto was, "Expect great things from God; attempt great things for God."

But Philip was like us. He expected nothing, and he attempted nothing in this case. He was so busy finding excuses for not carrying out Christ's concerns that he attempted nothing. We, too, figure without God! No wonder we think we cannot do anything. But with Him, we can do more than we dream. "With God, all things are possible."

There was a woman volunteer worker at a mental hospital who was performing a real service. After a brief time, she resigned because she was so depressed by seeing the mentally ill for a few hours one day a week. She admitted she simply did not have the resources to endure her work. Of course she didn't; none of us do. Our own strength is too feeble, but Jesus Christ makes up the difference. The woman volunteer, like Philip, had figured without God.

Many wives and husbands are at the point of refusing to put up with any weakness or immaturity in their partners. They know they should stay together as husband and wife, but they think they do not have the resources. Of course they do not. None of us do, alone, but there is a Helper who can perform miracles through us. Philip's failure is the failure of us all. We forget Christ, and we do not or will not take Him into account.

Jesus asked how many loaves they had and Philip showed Him five loaves and two fishes. Five loaves and two small fishes. What could they do for the crowds that sat on the hillside? What difference can such a little bit make when there is so much to be done?

We ask: "What difference do I make?" "What difference does my vote make at election time?" "What difference does my small contribution make to the church?" "What difference does my presence make on Sunday morning among three or four hundred?"

But the five loaves and two fishes were used by Jesus to accomplish a miracle. Exactly what happened, we are not certain. Some think it was a miracle of sharing—that lunch of fishes and loaves made everyone share with everyone else. In any case, Christ did much with little.

You think your talents, your time, your money and your presence mean little? With God, they mean much! Be so "practical" that you expect great things from Christ and attempt great things for Him!

Philip was a lot like us in another way: he had to be shown. His motto was "seeing is believing." He expressed a modern, scientific outlook on the night of the Last Supper. Jesus had been telling The Twelve about God our Father, and He explained that God had sent Him to show the Father's love.

Philip interrupted. "Show us the Father," he challenged. Philip was a skeptic. He wanted a specially-granted, private miracle or proof of God.

In Alaska, I knew a man named Hank who was that way. Hank and I were on the bull gang together in the gold fields one summer. We used to talk about religion frequently, and Hank said he would believe in God if he could only *see* some proof or miracle.

A lot of us will not admit it, but that is what we really want. We want a special revelation so that we can be absolutely certain of God. We ask for something we can *see*, or *hear*, or *touch.*

But if we need some kind of a little "clincher" to justify our faith, what kind of a faith would we have?

What kind of a God would we have from the "proofs" our little minds might conjure? God would be no bigger than our little minds!

Furthermore, what kind of a faith would we have if it were dependent upon "clinchers"? It would not be faith without the romance of asking, waiting, trusting. Ours would be a pat, cold, mechanical existence.

We are wrong to demand some extra "proof" for our own satisfaction before we can believe or accept a vital faith. As if a private little vision were needed, when God has already poured out His life on a Cross for us and raised up Christ from the dead! What more can we ask? What more must He do? What more do we want?

Jesus patiently answered Philip. "Have I been so long time with you, and yet hast thou not known me, Philip? . . . Believest thou not that I am in the Father and the Father in me? . . . He that hath seen me hath seen the Father. . . ."

We are slow to learn, for we are skeptics at heart. Even we who confess the divinity of Jesus Christ will not take Jesus seriously enough to realize that we know God when we know Jesus. Too often, we think of God as some*thing* or some*one* completely different from Jesus. But it is amazingly simple: know Jesus, and you know God.

Do not forget that Jesus called to a person like us and made him one of The Twelve. *In spite of his shortcom-*

ings, Philip the skeptical, Philip the practical, was a man Jesus regarded and needed as one of the Twelve Apostles.

Philip, in his own quiet, practical and sometimes skeptical way, was amazingly effective in bringing others to Jesus. In fact, wherever else he is mentioned in the New Testament, Philip is introducing someone to Jesus.

For example, it was Philip who spoke of Jesus to a fellow-skeptic named Nathanael. Nathanael speculated whether anyone good could come out of Nazareth. Philip knew that no one ever argued anyone into the presence of God, for although you may win the argument, you usually lose the man. Philip merely told Nathanael to come and see for himself.

"Come and see for yourself" is the perfect answer for anyone. In spite of our inadequacies, whatever they are—skepticism, lack of faith, or what have you—God has work for each of us.

We have all read the impressive statistics about church attendance and membership, and we know it is now at an all-time high. But the reports also disclose sixty-four million people in this country without any church affiliation. This means we still have a long way to go. So many are waiting to be invited—"Come and see for yourself." We can find a fair number of them in any of our communities.

Sure, you have inadequacies and imperfections, but no one is asking you to run off to a seminary and turn your collar around. Christ is only asking for you as you are. As you are, in spite of your lack of faith and your doubts, *expect* great things from Him. *Attempt* great things for Him.

NATHANAEL

6

Nathanael

THE WORLD SAW Nathanael as a cynic. He knew all the answers, he had friends, but even they saw him as a scoffer.

One day, a friend rushed up, greatly excited. "We have found the Messiah! We have found the One of whom Moses in the Law and the prophets wrote—Jesus of Nazareth!"

Nathanael merely sneered. "Can anything good come out of Nazareth?"

Nazareth! What a laugh! It was a couple of miles from where Nathanael, son of Tolmai, had grown up. (Bartholomew, Nathanael's full name, means simply "Son of Tolmai.") Nathanael knew Nazareth, a country village back in the hills. The Messiah from that place? Nothing happened there. The big things happened down in Jerusalem, or so Nathanael thought.

The truth is that God often uses the local and commonplace for the biggest things on earth. It is in the local and commonplace that God has repeatedly confronted men. He sent Jesus to be born in a local, commonplace stable. He let Jesus grow up in a local, commonplace, peasant home.

Jesus, too, used the local and commonplace. He took local, commonplace bread and wine for the most sacred and meaningful service we know—the Lord's Supper. He died on a local, commonplace piece of timber fixed as a cross upon another timber.

Maybe all that others have seen in you is the cynic. Maybe you have laughed or sneered at the local or commonplace. Maybe you have been seeking God, thinking there must be an exciting, dramatic, sensational experience. If you are, you may as well quit now. God does not reveal Himself in that way. It is through the day-by-day things that God works.

Perhaps you think all the big things happen in Washington, New York, Hollywood. They do not. The biggest things are happening in Mt. Lebanon, Bridgeville, or Prairie Corners, or wherever you live.

You may think something big and dazzling must happen to your youngsters to help them learn Christianity. No. Christianity is learned in the local and commonplace, in the everyday activities in your own home.

Many of us sneer at the local and commonplace. Sophisticated, educated and experienced as we think we are, we are often a bit inclined to be cynical. Maybe that is what the world sees in you: a cynic; a know-it-all. But God always sees you as something more than the world sees. Never measure yourself by what the world thinks of you. Think of yourself as how God thinks of you, for He sees a lot more.

Take Nathanael, for instance. The world saw him as a cynic. Jesus saw a cynic—and something more. That very morning, Jesus had passed an arbor and had casually looked inside. He saw a man earnestly reading his Bible and praying. The man thought he could not be seen, and no one but Jesus knew that the man secretly searching and wrestling for a real faith was Nathanael, the man the world knew as a cynic.

Somehow, a friend finally got Nathanael to meet Jesus. Jesus did not care what the world saw, for He saw a man who had qualities that the world did not realize. Anyone who could seriously study and meditate and pray and think, as this man was doing, was searching hard. Here was a man of conviction, intelligence, sincerity and depth.

Jesus talked with him. He befriended Nathanael and brought out what the world—and perhaps even Nathanael—never knew was in him. Nathanael eventually became one of the Twelve Disciples, the inner circle of friends and companions of Christ.

Jesus sees in you what the world has perhaps missed. He sees in you what you never dreamed existed. You may have thought you were only a cynical, hard-headed, hard-driving, hard-drinking businessman. Maybe you think of yourself as only a shallow-minded neurotic, or as just another housewife with never enough time to do all you should, or be all you should. The world might look upon you as just another tired mother with a shrill voice.

Christ sees you in a different light. He sees the *potential* in you, *the person you can become*, the person He can bring out in you! What the world saw: a cynic; what Jesus saw: a disciple. Ditto for any of us.

Before Nathanael met Jesus, he saw in Him just a hick from Nazareth, a neighboring country carpenter. His friends knew there was no use arguing, and as long as Nathanael knew about Jesus only by hearsay, Nathanael would never see a Saviour. Finally, Nathanael came and saw for himself. When he did, he was a changed man.

Maybe God, or Jesus, means little to you. One time a person was going on at length about Christianity being questionable stuff. It obviously meant nothing to him. A very wise friend quietly pointed up to some stained glass windows of a church building. From the outside, the windows seemed grimy and grey-colored.

"Don't look like much, do they, from out here?" he said. The critic agreed.

"Now come with me." The wise friend led the way inside the church, and there, on the inside, the light was shining through the windows, bringing out all the gorgeous colors and rich patterns of a figure of Christ.

You have to be on the inside to see Him. If you can stand on the outside and discuss and argue about Him forever, He will mean little to you.

Get on the inside, into the fellowship of the church, if you are not an active member already.

Get on the inside, into the pages of the Bible, if you have not done so.

Get on the inside, into His presence, by getting on your knees and turning yourself over to Him, admitting you need His help and humbly asking for it.

Get on the inside, into an attitude of taking Him seriously.

Then you will see Him as more than just another man. You will find He is the Teacher, the Son of God and the King! Nathanael did!

But Nathanael was human. There came a time when the authorities put a cross on his Teacher. They drove his Son of God through the streets like a common criminal. They pounded spikes through the hands and feet of his King of Israel and let Him die.

Nathanael was scared, and fed up. The Teacher, the

Son of God, the King of Israel was dead, and the world again saw Nathanael, the cynic. He wandered to a fishermen's town in Capernaum up north on Galilee. He signed on a boat with some other former followers of the dead Teacher, Son of God, King of Israel.

There, he should have lived out his years in obscurity. He constantly hoped that the Roman secret police would not track him down as one who had been with Jesus, and he hoped everybody would stop making remarks about following Jesus. He hoped he could forget the bright and wonderful years when he had known real living as a follower of Jesus.

A few nights after arriving in Capernaum, he was out all night fishing with some friends. They had no luck. They were tired, disgusted and discouraged.

Grey streaks were showing over the Syrian hills when they finally pulled toward shore. As they neared the shore, a voice called to them, and through the haze and darkness, they saw a man. A few seconds later, to their amazement, they saw it was Jesus, alive again.

Now let us stop and think about this for a minute. *They claimed they saw Jesus alive again.* This report could only be one of three things: either they made it up themselves; or it was an hallucination of some sort; or it was as they insisted, Jesus lived again. Let us take a closer look at these possibilities.

Had they invented the story that they had seen Jesus

alive? Hardly, since they were not expecting to see Him. Furthermore, what did they have to gain from such a lie? Nothing. As a matter of fact, they had everything to lose by announcing they had seen the Risen Lord. Laughed at, ridiculed, hounded, punished, and finally killed—that is what happened to most of them.

Hallucination? Hardly, with such a hard-working, down-to-earth group as the disciples. Take Nathanael, cynical and skeptical by nature, a student and a thinker, emotionally stable. He was not at all the type to be swept away by a phantom, or hallucinations.

The only possible way we can explain it is the way Nathanael and the others explained it: Jesus had been raised from the dead! That is what Nathanael believed.

The resurrection taught Nathanael that cynicism is not the last word. It convinced Nathanael that God is still on the scene, and taught Nathanael that God's love cannot be nullified or cut off. Nathanael went on to become one of the pillars in the founding of the Christian church.

If God had not raised Christ from the dead, cynicism would be the last word. There would be little point in our being here. There would not be much point in trying to live for something, or much point in anything at all.

But He is alive! And because He lives, we shall live also!

MATTHEW

7

Matthew

HIS NAME WAS Levi. He was a publican. That does not mean much to you, does it? Well, it meant a lot in Jesus' time. A publican was a tax collector. He had the social status of a bootlegger, a gambler, or one of the underworld among us today.

You ought to know about publicans. To begin with, they bought the office. As such, they were responsible for turning in to Rome a certain amount of taxes each year. Anything they collected above that amount was pure gravy for them. And how the publicans loved that gravy!

Levi had the choice position of tax collector in Capernaum, on the busy Damascus-Acre trade route. Levi must have grown enormously wealthy.

All publicans grew wealthy. They bought the lucrative office, but when they did, they sold their consciences. They had to, if they were going to keep their jobs. They couldn't be honest. Graft, fraud, greed, extortion—they were soon covered with unbelievable corruption.

A publican bought a lucrative office, and sold out his companions. He lost all his friends because they feared a taxgatherer. Others had only hatred for a tax collector. A publican could not get any respect or esteem from the Romans who looked down on local taxgatherers as useful tools. Taxgatherers were driven to hanging around with the rich scum nobody liked.

A publican bought a lucrative office, and sold out his country. Taxes represented the burdens of occupation by hostile power, and anyone who played along with Rome was hated as a traitor. Tax collectors were regarded as such low scoundrels that their testimony was not acceptable in the courts, and they were not allowed to take oaths. Nobody would believe them.

They bought the lucrative office, and sold out their church. "Tax collectors and harlots" was the phrase for the lowest order on the ladder of respectable society. A publican was assumed to be so unscrupulous and unethical that he was not even allowed in the church. His money was believed tainted and was not accepted by any synagogue.

In other words, being a publican was more than having

an occupation. It was a reputation! Such a man was Levi.

But Jesus saw in this man what no one else saw. He picked Levi as a follower, and even made him one of the Twelve Disciples!

It was not very smart public relations on Jesus' part, we might say. After all, there were plenty of men with good recommendations, respectable backgrounds and good credentials. Why did He pick Levi? The crowds were horrified. Why did He not pick someone in high public esteem to help His cause? Practically anyone but Levi might have added to Jesus' personal popularity and the popularity of His cause.

But Jesus did not come to gain popularity. He came to show what God can do with the most unlikely cases. Levi is a prize example.

Jesus gave Levi a new name. From then on, Levi called himself "Matthew," which means simply "gift of God." Any of you who are named Matthew or Theodore or Dorothy will be interested to know you are carrying a badge meaning "God's gift." Hopefully, you are living in such a way that you fulfill the name's meaning.

Matthew did. His life from that moment was truly "a gift from God." Matthew, the man with a past, had found God and had been found by God: Jesus Christ had come into his life. He did something about it right away. If Christ really gets hold of anyone, that person wants to do something. He wants to have others know Christ.

Matthew had an original and imaginative way of discipleship. Privilege means responsibility, and for Matthew, the privilege of following Christ was the responsibility of telling others about Him.

For Matthew, this meant arranging a dinner at which all his rich outcast cronies could meet Jesus. He gave a dinner, not a pious prayer meeting or vague "Come around to church sometime. . . ." Matthew had a fresh approach which Jesus liked.

There was nothing sanctimonious about Matthew, and there never need be anything sanctimonious about any Christian. There certainly never was with Jesus. He went to the dinner, and was friendly toward all the shady characters, even though His behavior shocked many of the self-righteous and sanctimonious.

Christ likes the imaginative, practical approach of businessmen like Matthew and people like you. The important thing is to share your faith in Him with others. To keep it, you must give it away.

Matthew's party was for rich outcasts. We often think outcasts are always on skid row, but there are many rich outcasts around us. Many people who are materially "well off" are outcasts from God, or outcasts from society—or even outcasts from themselves.

Do something about the ones you know. Be specific and be definite because you know they need God's help.

Ask them if you can pick them up for church next Sunday.

Another thing Matthew did was to turn over his abilities to Jesus Christ. Matthew had put in some years with the Roman "bureau of internal revenue." He was familiar with Roman regard for order and he was a sharp businessman with an adding-machine mind. He had a knack for putting down the facts straight. He could arrange things in neat, orderly ways. He had an observant eye for detail. He was a note-taker with a carefully trained memory. All these abilities were useful to a good businessman. He now used them for God's business.

Matthew's restless pen wrote down the gospel which bears his name. It marks such an orderly transition from the Old Testament to the New Testament that it has always stood first in the list of twenty-seven books of the New Testament.

Matthew never figures much in the public eye. Apparently, he was not in the spotlight as much as the others. But not everyone must be! Thank God for the Matthews who simply turn over their abilities and talents to Christ.

Think of how much we owe Matthew, the disciple. Were it not for him, we would not have a record of the Sermon on the Mount. He must have been there quietly taking notes, jotting down Jesus' words.

Were it not for Matthew, we might not understand

why Jesus stressed what a man must *do* to be a Christian. Matthew knew all the tricks in the book, for he had been one of the worst offenders. Because he knew human nature, he is the one who stresses what Jesus expects of a follower. Matthew puts it on the line and talks straight to people like us who need straight speaking: "No man can serve two masters . . . Ye cannot serve God and mammon . . . Seek ye first the kingdom of God. . . ." God or gold? First things first.

Matthew, the man with a past and the man with talents, used both for Christ's work. Thanks to both, with God's help, he truly became a "gift of God."

For all of this, Matthew learned and kept his humility. Although others tried to forget his past, Matthew never tried to hide it. In fact, he insisted on referring to himself throughout his gospel as "the publican." Everyone else was charitable. They all were for burying the fact that Matthew had been Levi, the Publican. Matthew humbly and stubbornly used it as his signature.

Apparently he never forgot what he had been, and he never forgot what Jesus had done for him. He was anxious to have everyone know. A publican! His readers would have been revolted. But Christ changed even him! Matthew says in effect, "What better proof could you want of His claims than *me*?"

"Sick and sinful men, come to Him," Matthew pleads. "He made me a new man. He can do the same for you!"

It seems significant that Matthew puts the story of his own conversion in the middle of a section on miracles. He is telling how Jesus healed a woman of palsy. Then he relates that Jesus gave sight to two blind men. Matthew then slips in another miracle: how he was saved–saved from himself, saved from his greed.

How about a miracle in your life? An unlikely case, you say? Ah yes, but that is just the type Christ unexpectedly makes into Christians.

Your real destiny is to be His. Why not start now?

THOMAS

8

Thomas

On January 1, 1929, California Institute of Technology was playing in the Rose Bowl against Georgia Tech. In the opening seconds, Georgia Tech received. The player was hit hard by tacklers from California; so hard, in fact, that the ball squirted out of his arms, and right into the outstretched hands of the California center named Roy Riegels.

Riegels started down the field. As three Tech players came at him, he reversed his field. Then he cut the other way and circled. Suddenly he saw the opening he had been seeking and went for pay dirt. Yard after yard flew by.

The fans were screaming, for Riegels was running in

the wrong direction! He covered sixty-three yards before he was finally brought down by one of his own teammates. Riegels' blunder set up Georgia Tech and won the game for them.

Poor Riegels was never allowed to forget. He is still remembered as the man who ran the wrong way. When he married, became a father, was lost in a snowstorm, he was referred to years later as (and to this day is known as) "Wrong Way" Riegels. The tag will probably always be around his neck.

Another man has a tag around his neck. His name is Thomas, but he is usually referred to as "Doubting Thomas," or "Thomas the Doubter." We almost sneer when we say his name, and imply he was a near-villain, a contemptuous type. Thomas had his good points, and although man has a fickle memory, God remembers. Maybe we recall only the bad sides, or the unfortunate acts, but God remembers much more.

Maybe you have been carrying a name, or trying to live down a reputation, or are known as a person with a past. That may be the part of your life that others remember, but God remembers everything. He gives you a new start.

Thomas had his good points: for example, take the time Jesus wanted to visit His friend Lazarus who was deathly sick in Bethany. Bethany is only over the hill from Jerusalem, but Jesus was such a marked man that

He would risk arrest if He got near Jerusalem again.

The disciples objected to the journey because it was unsafe, but Thomas caught a glimpse of Jesus' character that the others had missed. He saw that Jesus did not come to save Himself, but to serve and help others. He saw that Jesus *could* live out His years in security and safety in quiet Galilee, but Thomas knew Jesus did not regard His mission as the preservation of His own life. It was quite simple: Lazarus needed help; Jesus could give that help; Jesus was going to go.

Thomas said, in effect, "Very well, let us go. The man needs help, and our Master can help him. If it means stoning—well that is part of the cost. Let us go!" We need more people with the "let us go!" attitude. Good old Thomas! He saw all the dangers, but he still said, "Let us go"

Anybody can be an excuse-maker; we are all experts at that. But when we see someone who needs help, or a situation that needs remedying, how often can we say, "Let us go!"?

We complain about the school situation or politics. We need some Thomases to come along and say "Let's go!"

We gripe about juvenile delinquency, and turn the air stale with our words on the subject. We need more who will say, "Let us go" and get to work in a scout troop, or teach in a church school.

We complain about the future of the world and the coming generation. We need more parents to say "Let's go!" on the serious business of spending time and teaching Christianity to children.

We need more young people who will say, "Let's go!" and use their talents and drive and education to become agricultural experts, engineers, nurses, doctors, and so on, in the mission field, or in the ministry.

Don't think, however, that you must blow bugles to be a disciple. Thomas was a plain-spoken, straight-thinking man. Like us, he was often seriously perplexed. But Jesus still needed him and wanted him as one of The Twelve.

Thomas was perplexed when Jesus spoke after the Last Supper. "In my Father's house are many mansions: if it were not so, I would have told you. I go to prepare a place for you. And if I go . . . I will come again, and receive you unto myself; that where I am, there ye may be also. And whither I go ye know, and the way ye know. . . ." Father's house? Many mansions? The way? Thomas didn't "get it," and he said so. How could he know the way? What did it all mean?

That is the question we still ask: How can we know the way? The problems of living are tremendously confusing, and our personal problems are terrifyingly confusing. What is the way?

Jesus answered, "I am the way, the truth, and the life." *The* way—not a way, one of several—but *the way.* In other words, Jesus is the answer. Know Him and you know God's plans. You know God!

We owe a big debt to Thomas. His questions were blunt, but Jesus never dodged them. In answer to Thomas' questions, Jesus came out with some of His most forthright statements about Himself.

"I am the way, the truth, and the life." I am grateful for Thomas, because if it had not been for plain-speaking Thomas, we might not have had this banner of a line.

I am even glad Thomas doubted the fact that Jesus rose from the dead. It has helped an obstinate, hard-headed skeptic like me to believe. If it could be believed by a hard-headed obstinate man like Thomas, who was there at the time, it must be true.

For some reason, Thomas had not been with the others when Jesus was first seen after the crucifixion. Jesus had even eaten a piece of fish to show the disciples they were not seeing a vision or a psychological phenomenon of some sort.

They reported all this to Thomas. Impossible, he replied. He knew too well the details of a crucifixion: the sickening sight of a human body hanging on a ghastly cross; the stench; the flies; the blood; the sounds of death. The evidence was overwhelming and no man could possibly survive that! A crucified man was finished!

"I will not believe. Except I shall see in his hands the print of the nails, and put my finger into the print of the nails . . . I will not believe." Thomas was emphatic. These are the words of a man who would have made a good attorney today.

Many people dismiss the resurrection story as a hoax, or others pass it off as something unsubstantiated and reported by unreliable people, or overemotional souls. But here is Thomas. He and the other followers were not easily persuaded simpletons. They were not spiritualists at a seance, believing what they want to see, and what they make up in their own minds.

Thomas and the others were rugged, out-of-doors, working men. Like any such people, and like us, they had a keen sense of fact. Thomas and the others lived close to the ground. They were not the flighty, excitable, imaginative type.

Look at the facts as they are reported in the gospels. Jesus appeared another time, when Thomas was present. Jesus, the Risen Lord, went directly to Thomas. "Reach thither thy hand," He said, "and thrust it into my side." Thomas fell to his knees, gasping, "My Lord and my God." Jesus said, "Blessed are they that have not seen, and yet have believed."

Thomas became a changed man. Tradition claims

that he went to India, taking the good news of the resurrection. Rumor also has it that Thomas died in India. Maybe these persistent traditions have never been proven or disproven, but they are in keeping with Thomas' personality. They are in keeping with what usually happens when a man takes the resurrection seriously.

We should be glad Thomas doubted, because it helps to clinch it in our minds that Jesus *did* rise from the dead. That fact means everything in the world: hope of victory, forgiveness, and life everlasting.

SIMON THE ZEALOT

9

Simon the Zealot

THE BIBLE DOES not tell us much about Simon the Zealot. He is another of the quiet, unobtrusive people who must have been around helping Christ, and who, thank God!, are still around now.

Simon—*the Zealot*. His name identifies him as a member of the party of Zealots, who in Jesus' time, were a band of guerrilla fighters pledged to drive out the Romans. They functioned as a sort of Jewish underground and kept the country on the edge of open revolt most of the time. The Zealots were from Jesus' neighborhood, Galilee. Many fellow Jews disliked the Zealots and the Romans of course tried to stamp them out.

Simon, the Zealot! He must have been an interesting

man! I have met members of various underground organizations and they were of an unusual breed. I stayed a few days in Ireland with a man in Limerick who had been active in guerrilla operations against Britain back in 1916. I have met members of the Dutch, Norwegian, French and Belgian undergrounds of World War II. They are fascinating individuals.

They have several things in common, I have noticed: they are men who seek a cause for which to live; they are men who want to change things; they are men who do not fit into the usual molds; they are men who like adventure in life.

Simon the Zealot, I am certain, was such a man: a man who wanted a cause in life; a man who wanted to change things; a man who was different; a man who liked adventure in life. He, too, is like us!

We are men and women who want a cause for which to live. We are thinking people and I know that every one of us realizes the folly and futility of living for self. We must have some idea or ideal for which we can live and die. We do not become emotional about it or make a public issue of it, but that is the way we are.

For example, a man once sat in my study and told me his story: good job; owned a home and car; nice wife, and so on. He seemed very much ashamed, however, to tell me that during the war he really got more out of life than at any other time. He had been a pilot and had thoroughly enjoyed it. He had loved the life because he had thrown himself into it.

It was really quite simple. During the war, he had a cause to live for, and now he had none. In spite of his new "Olds," nice home and all the rest, he was unhappy. We must have a cause in our lives.

On a hot July Sunday afternoon, I passed a group of volunteer firemen. Please note that they were *volunteer* firemen. These men were dressed in clumsy, heavy firemen's boots, sweating under a merciless sun, cleaning some sections of firehose. And they were enjoying it!

They had a cause: it was their fire department; they believed in it; it was greater than they were. To them it was important enough to rouse them out of their hammocks on a steaming Sunday afternoon.

Simon had a cause: the Zealots—until he met Jesus Christ. We all belong to various causes, and most of them serve a good purpose. However, only one cause is really worthwhile enough to ask and hold your complete allegiance: the cause of Jesus Christ. Only His cause is big enough to ask and hold your wholehearted devotion!

We are men and women who want to change things. Simon the Zealot also was such a person. He was dissatisfied with present conditions, and he joined the Zealots. He gave the group every ounce of his support because he believed the underground could change things.

I have often wondered why Simon switched his allegiance from the powerful guerrilla group which seemed to be accomplishing big things. Why did he leave the Zealots and join an unarmed carpenter from Nazareth?

There is only one answer: Jesus was doing more. Jesus was producing real, lasting changes, and His kingdom was the lasting one. Jesus must have impressed this sensitive, dissatisfied young Zealot named Simon.

How about you? Most of you are Simons. You have a keen social conscience, and you are dissatisfied with present conditions. You want to help. You want to change things in our world. Many groups and organizations are trying to change things, but only one lives on: the church of Jesus Christ. All others are man-made and have a limited period of usefulness.

If you want to change things, enlist for service under the cause of Jesus Christ. He has changed more people, changed more history, influenced more lives than anything or anyone before or since.

Without money, without arms, He has conquered more millions than Alexander, Caesar, Mohammed, Napoleon or Hitler. Without our emphasis on science and learning, He shed more light on things human and divine than all the philosophers and scholars combined.

Without formal eloquence, He spoke words of life such as were never spoken before, or since, and produced effects beyond the reach of orator and poet. Without writing a single line, He has set more pens in motion and furnished themes for more sermons, orations, discussions, works of art, learned volumes and great music than the whole army of great men of ancient and modern times.

We are men who want some adventure in life. Simon, I'm certain, was a man in search of adventure. You have to want a generous dash of adventure to tie up with the underground, and there was adventure galore with the Zealots. It is easy to imagine Simon slipping out of his house at midnight; dodging silently through deserted, dark back streets; avoiding Roman sentries; climbing the wall and dropping down; crouching for a minute to listen; then dashing to the cover of an olive grove; stopping again; lying flat on the ground for minutes to make sure no one had detected him and was trailing him. Then, heart beating quickly, scrambling crosscountry over the desolate moors and hills; down a long steep ravine; a password; a forced march; a silent but bloody strike on a dozing Roman outpost.

Let no one ever think that life was tame for Simon the Zealot! This was his life, and he lived it to the full, until he met someone even more adventuresome. And *this* Adventurer had even a greater challenge to offer.

If you think that Jesus Christ is dull, boring, safe, tame and grey, it is only because some misguided Christians have made Him seem that way. Do not judge *Him* by *them!* Simon certainly found Jesus the most adventuresome man he ever knew, and following Him the best adventure he ever experienced. We can find the same things in Jesus, for He still is the most challenging, interesting, red-blooded man ever known. Everyone else looks pale and dull compared to Him.

The Christian life is the most adventuresome action man knows, although we often mistakenly think that our various forms of selfishness and sin are really exciting, and that Christianity is insipid. Actually, selfishness and sin are sickeningly dull, and soon become bits of putrefying grey carrion.

Jesus Christ is the most alive personality around us. Following Him is without a doubt the most truly adventuresome thing anyone can do. Try it for yourself and see!

Perhaps you think you are different. "I'm not the type. How could I ever have anything to do with all this Christianity? I'm not a religious man. . . ." Neither was Simon the Zealot.

It seems impossible that Simon the Zealot and Matthew the Publican could belong to the same group of twelve men. One of the vows that Simon had taken as a Zealot was to kill a tax collector such as Matthew. Yet here were a potential murderer and a potential victim in the same intimate group. The tax hater and the tax-gatherer: the patriot who fought the foreign power, and the traitor who sold out to the foreign power! Side by side.

A Simon who had been a Zealot and a Matthew who had been a taxgatherer are only two examples of how Jesus can transform and use *any* man. If you are not already, you are bound to be His some day.

THADDAEUS

10

Thaddaeus

THERE WAS ONCE a man who had two nicknames. His real name was Judas, son of James, but he usually went by one of his two nicknames. One of these nicknames was Lebbaeus, which translated "hearty" or "the hearty one." His other nickname is the name we most often use: Thaddaeus. Thaddaeus means "the courageous one" or "bold."

Nicknames usually give some indication of a man's character, and people do not bestow nicknames such as "hearty" or "the bold" unless there is a good reason. How did Judas, son of James, pick up his nicknames? Consider his nickname Thaddaeus, "The Bold." Had he rescued a boatload of men on a stormy night on Galilee? Was he known as an exceptionally brave seaman? Was he a man who had not been afraid to stand up to Rome?

The nickname Lebbaeus, "The Hearty," implies he was good company—a friendly, affable person, a man who got a big kick out of life. Lebbaeus was a man who threw himself into living life to the hilt. He was a robust extrovert who liked people and life, a man who would have made a good salesman or a personnel man, or a toastmaster.

Maybe you think Jesus Himself was a harmless dreamer who cannot be taken seriously, and who holds no appeal. Just remember, however, that He held so much appeal that a man who was nicknamed "The Hearty" and "The Courageous" left everything to spend all his time with Jesus.

Maybe you have thought Christianity was for old women and old men. Not the way Jesus and His followers lived it! Judas, son of James, was hardly *that* type.

Judas, the son of James, better known as "The Hearty" and "The Bold," was just the man Jesus wanted as one of His closest friends and most trusted companions. In fact, Jesus called this man to be one of the Twelve Apostles.

For two or three years, Judas, son of James, better known as Thaddaeus or Lebbaeus, lived with the others who were Jesus' inner circle of followers. He did not distinguish himself in any way, particularly, but not everybody can be a hero.

He must have been tremendously impressed and thrilled by Jesus, especially in the last days of Jesus' life. Palm Sunday had been a dramatic occasion. People sang and shouted and cheered for Jesus, palm branches and cloaks were strewn on the road for Him, and Jesus' name was on the lips of everyone in Jerusalem. This was the way Thaddaeus loved it: applause, parades, and popularity for Jesus. The kingdom was really on its way, he figured.

Then a day or so later in the Temple courtyard, Jesus strode in, deliberately picked up the end of a long, heavy table used by the money changers, and spilled everything to the pavement. Then He moved to the animal market and knotting a piece of cord into a thong, He drove out the herds of milling, noisy sheep, goats, oxen and other livestock. The crowds were stunned, then delighted. Deafening cheers, talk of a revolution, of making Jesus King, of His being the long awaited Messiah! What a day it was for Thaddaeus. He liked excitement and action, and Jesus was giving him plenty of both.

Then, abruptly, all Jesus' public appearances stopped, and there were no more dazzling displays of daring. What had happened to Jesus? He had won over the whole population. He had campaigned brilliantly for the nomination, convinced everyone, had everyone ready to vote for Him, and then He had yawned and walked away disinterested. Or, so it seemed to Thaddaeus.

When Jesus called The Twelve together for an intimate supper, which He told them would be His last, Thaddaeus was impatient. Even when the other Judas, the infamous Judas Iscariot, went out to betray Jesus, Thaddaeus was fidgety. He listened as Jesus quietly instructed them, His followers, to carry on for Him. Thaddaeus listened, growing more and more annoyed. Finally, he heard Jesus saying that He would be killed, and that did it. Thaddaeus had had enough.

He blurted out an interruption. Why all this talk to the disciples in private? Why did not Jesus go out to make His public appearances, as He had a few days earlier, and convince everyone He *was* the Messiah? There was no sense in taking all this trouble just to talk with His followers around a table.

Judas, son of James, "The Hearty" and "The Bold," had three necessary lessons to learn.

1) *He learned patience with God.* God works in His own good time. Often our timetable is not His, and there are delays for our own good. Often He says "No" for a long time. If you are like me, you are often like Thaddaeus. You try to stampede God to carry out *your* little plans immediately. But who are we to tell Him how to do anything?

Suppose while you were at work tomorrow morning,

some brash youngster walked up to you, took a look at what you were doing and proceeded to tell you how to do your job. You know very well how you would feel and what you would think of that youngster. That is exactly the way we often behave toward God!

Not too long ago, Jock, my youngster, brought me his steamshovel, which was in bad need of a repair job. We took it downstairs to the workbench and looked it over to see what could be done. It was obviously going to take a little time and a little work, but Jock had a hundred suggestions on how to do the job in thirty seconds. A bit of glue would hold the metal arm in place, he thought. After one minute, he was very restless and growing increasingly impatient. By the end of five minutes, he stormed away angrily, claiming that his steamshovel was broken and that I could not fix it. How often we behave that way toward God—trying to rush Him, trying to instruct Him.

Christ always knew exactly what He was doing, and He scheduled things precisely right. God is like Jesus.

2) *Thaddaeus learned obedience to Christ.* Judas, the son of James, wanted to be a spectator. He wanted to sit in the box seat on the sidelines and watch God do all the playing. God does not want watchers, spectators or a cheering section. He wants *obedient men.*

Frequently we hear people ask, "Why doesn't God *do* something?" They are never very specific about what they want Him to do—just so *He* does *something*. They usually speak in a tone of voice which implies they think God had better get hustling pretty fast, and whip up a couple of good, impressive miracles to change things. War, for example: Why doesn't God end international strife? Famine, to cite another case: Why doesn't God do something about that?

The truth of the matter is that God usually works through obedient men and women. Wars are man-caused, and when we and our leaders can learn to obey God, at least some of our international tension can be avoided. Famine? Man-caused again. But there are also surpluses in our world, and obedient men and women will see to it that we pass some of our abundance down the table to those who are hungry.

Another question people keep bringing up is "Why don't I *feel* anything?" which is an expression of a popular and dangerous idea that we must *feel* something before we can have any religion. We have the mistaken idea that unless our feelings are aroused, something is wrong. We expect an emotional charge or spiritual jag, and if we do not experience anything inside, we feel a bit guilty, resentful and frustrated. This idea may come from some of the religious trash people are reading these days. Literature which may appear religious is not necessarily true. Christ is still *the* way, *the* truth, *the* life!

Too many of us are worshiping feeling instead of worshiping God. If you are looking for only a feeling, you may look for a long time, because Jesus did not come to give a little warm glow inside. He came to demand all-out obedience. He called for obedience, and promised life.

3) *Thaddaeus learned responsibility to Christ.* Judas, the Hearty and Bold, was all for Christianity. He wanted it to apply to everyone—except himself. How like all of us!

He finally learned that Christianity started with Him before it was going to mean a thing in his own life. No matter how many Christians there are in the world, no matter how many church-goers there are in the United States, no matter how many churches there are in your town, Christianity will never mean a thing in your life until Jesus Christ has meaning for you personally. Until you have come to terms with Him, Christianity will never, can never, amount to much as far as you are concerned.

We cannot shift Christianity off to someone else. It is our responsibility. It starts with you personally, and with me personally. We are responsible to Christ for doing His work, extending His love and bringing to others His forgiveness, and we cannot pass on this responsibility to anyone else. Someone asks, "It was easy for people to believe in Christ when they saw Him raised from the dead, but how can people believe now?" Answer: outsiders know Him through us. Our responsibility to Him is to live so that others can know Him.

What happens when a person learns patience with God, obedience to Him, and responsibility to Him? Jesus has a plain, direct answer. He makes His home with that person, and God becomes a personal Friend and Helper. That person *can* be you!

We are not exactly sure what happened to Judas, son of James, nicknamed Thaddaeus and Lebbaeus. The Bible is interested in telling the story of Jesus, not the biographies of men. But apparently Christ's life was very much in the life of Judas. He is most commonly remembered simply as the disciple, Thaddaeus, or the nickname which means "The Courageous One."

There is a legend that has persisted down through the years in the Greek church that Thaddaeus went up to the wilds of what is now northeast Turkey and southern Russia. There, the legend says, he lived up to his nickname by courageously healing the sick and even nursing a leper. He was courageous to the end and is supposed to have died from the arrow wounds inflicted by a hostile mob in the town of Ararat. It is only tradition, of course, but it is consistent with what we would expect of Thaddaeus, a man in whom Christ had made His home.

Courage is not one of the long suits in most of us; courage to do the right thing, courage to take a stand, courage to go against the wishes of the crowd, courage to be Christ's man or woman. *Our fears are actually loneliness.* We panic at thinking we are a minority of one. We blanch at facing life, the world, friends or enemies, alone.

You need not be alone, for there is the invisible Ally at your side, with whom there is always a majority. Be patient with Him. Obey Him. Be responsible to Him and He will be at home in your life. Your nickname may not be Thaddaeus, but you are not alone, and you are not afraid. Christ lives in you!

JAMES, SON OF ALPHAEUS

11

James, Son of Alphaeus

THERE ONCE WAS a man about whom no one remembered much, years later. Mostly, people remembered his nickname and how he looked. When it came to writing about the times they had all lived through, no one bothered to record anything this man had said or done.

His name was James, son of Alphaeus. He lived in Jesus' times, but the Bible does not mention a solitary thing that James, son of Alphaeus, did or said. There is only his name. Yet Jesus thought so much of this man that He made him one of the Twelve Disciples!

We do not even know about his background. We do know he had a brother, Levi, son of Alphaeus. Levi, son of Alphaeus, was a man with a past—a traitorous, cheating tax collector. Levi, son of Alphaeus, became Matthew, the disciple of Jesus.

Was James, son of Alphaeus, a man like his brother? Did he meet Jesus through his brother, Matthew? Sometimes we forget the power of example we have over members of our own families. Maybe James met the Lord because of his brother's Christianity.

Or had the training he had certainly received in his home sunk in after all? Alphaeus, James' father, and Mary, James' mother, were devout folks who would have had a strong program of religious education in their home, and would have provided a high example for James and Matthew. Probably the parents' hearts were broken as they watched their boy Levi drift into the life of a tax collector. Maybe their hearts were broken a second time when James did the same.

Yet such training and example are never in vain. Like slowly maturing seeds that must be planted deeply, all the training and example of their home came to life in their boys' lives and bore fruit. Both Levi and James ended up as members of the disciple group of The Twelve.

Levi, or Matthew, of course is the famous one, the writer of the Gospel according to Matthew. His name stands well up on the list of disciples. James his brother, however, ends up at the end of the list, and James is generally forgotten. He was eclipsed not only by his more famous brother, but also by another James.

The other James in the group of disciples was James, the son of Zebedee. He was the member of the trio, Peter, James, and John, which gets all the limelight. This other James, son of Zebedee, was a fiery, outspoken hot-head. When James, son of Alphaeus, was mentioned, people had to be able to tell him apart from the more prominent James.

James, son of Alphaeus, must have been a short man, if we judge from his nickname which was James, "The Little," or something like "Little Jim," or "The Short James." Maybe it was Jesus who nicknamed him James "The Short." Jesus had a kindly sense of humor and dubbed more than one man with a nickname which stuck: Simon became Peter; Levi became Matthew.

James, "The Little." At first sight, he seems little in every way; nothing prominent about him. He is the forgotten disciple. No one ever preaches on this James. The Bible carries his name only in the lists of disciples, but he consistently appears in every list, including the list of those who were the nucleus of the earliest Christian church after the death and resurrection of Jesus. Yet, the mere fact that he is always mentioned as one of the Twelve Disciples shows conclusively that Jesus saw something in James the Little, and counted on him to make a distinctive contribution. James the Little, as one of The Twelve, shows the important role of the *quiet*, the *forgotten*, the *little* people in life. There have been so many of these people that we hardly know where to start for examples. All through history, the quiet, the forgotten and the little have done the most.

Back in the early 1200's, everybody knew Innocent III was the Pope. Back in the early 1200's, Innocent crowned Otto IV as Emperor of the Holy Roman Empire, and everybody knew about Otto IV. Back in the early 1200's everybody was talking about the Moslem leader, Saladin, and the Crusaders who were fighting him.

A quiet, little man who nursed a few lepers and helped the poor should have been forgotten. But today we remember *this* man—Francis of Assisi—and seldom wonder about Innocent the Third, or Otto the Fourth, or the Crusades.

In London, during the 1850's, there was a dry-goods clerk named George Williams who was a quiet, forgotten little man. George Williams never became Prime Minister of England, or even sat in Parliament. He never made any headlines, wrote any books, won any prizes, fought any battles or had any fuss made over him. All he did was invite a few young men to join him in prayer and Christian fellowship during their free hours. Although George Williams did not know it, he started something. Today we have the Young Men's Christian Association.

Never underestimate the influence of the forgotten, quiet, little people. They are actually the most prominent. If only a few other quiet, forgotten little people had been Jameses! A policeman, a railroad passenger and two railway officials, for example.

In South Africa, in 1893, a brown-skinned man bought a first-class railroad ticket to ride overnight to Pretoria. He went into a first-class compartment for the long ride. At Maritzburg, a white man came into the car, looked at the brown intruder and withdrew. A minute later, he reappeared with two railway officials who ordered the man to the baggage car. He showed his first-class ticket, but they said he had to leave. He stayed. A minute later, a policeman came in and threw the brown man and his baggage out on the station platform. That was the turning point in the brown man's life. He went back to India and became well-known in later years. You know his name: Mahatma Gandhi.

If only there were more Jameses in the world! A restaurant owner, for example. A restaurant man in South Carolina ordered a brown-skinned customer and his family to leave his restaurant one night. He probably never dreamed how disastrous the results would be, but he had so humiliated this man and his children that as soon as the man returned to South America, where he lived, he joined the Communist party and is now a leader of the Communists in South America. He attributes his new faith to that night in South Carolina.

If only there were more like James the Little in the world! A janitor, for example, on the evening a slum kid came into a Bowery settlement house. The janitor saw the boy by the door and because he did not like his looks, he told him to get out. Later, the world heard of that boy in Russia. He was one of the masterminds behind the October 1917 Revolution that put the Communists in power. His name was Leon Trotsky. Suppose someone had invited the boy in that evening, and befriended and helped him? (It makes me shudder when I think how I sometimes bounce the neighborhood problem child out of our yard!)

There was nothing very prominent about any of the people who so decisively affected lives the wrong way. It is just the old story: the quiet, little forgotten people like us are real forces in the world.

Too many men think that the parade to the kitchen to kiss the wife as they come home is trivial. I know many who complain they are too busy for their children. These little things, done or not done by these little people mean nothing, apparently. But think again. The insignificant is usually the most significant. The forgotten, the quiet and the little can be the dynamos for good, too.

The minister of the Presbyterian Church in Joplin, Missouri, several years ago saw a smudgy face pressed against the Church window. He ignored the greasy marks on the windows and walked over to see what the boy was looking at. It was only a map hanging on the wall, a leftover from a missionary society meeting. Most of us would have left things alone and gone home, or perhaps would have asked the boy to keep his dirty hands off the nice clean windows.

Instead, the minister asked the boy to come inside for a better look at the map, which illustrated Presbyterian mission stations throughout the world. The minister began explaining what the missionaries were doing and why they went out to all those places on the map. Finally he and the boy parted.

The boy grew up and the minister left Joplin, but something took hold in that boy. His name is Barney Morgan. For years, he was a missionary in Puerto Rico, and today, he is Secretary for the West Indies of the Board of National Missions of the Presbyterian Church, U.S.A. All because someone took a little time.

A giant of a youngster slouched into an Illinois schoolroom one day after school. The teacher, Mentor Graham, looked up and recognized the young husky standing there awkwardly as the new young buck who had recently moved to town and who had whipped the daylights out of all the local toughs. Graham looked up and down the six-foot-four-inches of muscle and ignorance before him and offered to help him read and to lend him a few books. No one remembers Mentor Graham nowadays. He was one of the quiet men, but his pupil will be remembered for a long time. His name was Abraham Lincoln.

A group of twenty or so people meet every Thursday evening in our church, and by all the rules I know, they should be either in the workhouse, the bughouse, or the cemetery. Yet, they are happy, hard-working people. They are all alcoholics, who, by the grace of God working through two or three quiet men, are alive and sane and well and sober and happy.

Headline stuff does not mean much. The people who really count are the quiet, forgotten little ones. They are the significant people doing the significant things.

You may think you are very insignificant or that you do not count for much or amount to much. As long as you are alive, remember that God has put you here for a purpose, and that purpose is to serve God and enjoy Him forever. In your everyday experience and routine, serving Him is the most significant thing in the world.

Anatole France, the novelist, was a sophisticated snob who was popular a few years back. He once sneered that men are always smaller than they seem to be. He was wrong. That is directly contrary to the purpose for which Jesus lived and died and rose again. We can be *bigger* than we seem to be!

Jesus called a quiet, little, forgotten man as a disciple. They called James, son of Alphaeus, James "The Little." Maybe he was little in height, little in fame and headlines and acclaim but he was big in mind, big in heart, and big in soul. Why? Because he belonged to Jesus Christ!

The world will not remember much about many of us one hundred years from now, and probably nothing about us five hundred years from now. But do not let that lead you to believe you are insignificant. You are already more significant than you dream.

Belong to Christ. With Him, you are bigger than you seem to be!

JUDAS ISCARIOT

12

Judas Iscariot

THE NAME JUDAS brings a shudder to us. It is a synonym for "traitor," and seems to symbolize the worst in treachery and deceit. We even call the stockyard animal that guides the others to the block "the Judas-goat."

Judas is the last name in the world we would ever give a child. It may come as a shock to us to learn, however, that the name Judas was once very popular. It was a proud name in Jewish history. Judah, or Judas, was the name of one of the twelve sons of Jacob in the Old Testament, and the brilliant uprising for independence in 164 B.C. was led by a man named Judas. This Judas, Judas Maccabaeus, was looked upon by all Jews as a sort of George Washington. Judas was a name of heroes.

Parents proudly named sons Judas. Jesus' parents even named one of Jesus' brothers Judas, or Jude (which are one and the same name). One other in the group of Twelve was named Judas (Judas, son of James, also known by his nicknames, "Lebbaeus" and "Thaddaeus"). It was a name parents were proud to give and a name men were proud to carry.

Probably a father and mother in the village of Kerioth, south of Jerusalem, were happy when a baby boy was born to them. Probably this same father and mother, being devout Jews, were anxious to give their child a name with meaning and tradition. Judas was a natural choice.

The implication from all this is that Judas had the advantage of a good home. He was probably raised like other Jewish boys with a thorough grounding in the Bible. So Judas grew up, to be known as the Judas from the village of Kerioth, or Judas Iscariot.

He apparently had no infamous past like Matthew before he met Jesus. He apparently had no vices that made him stand out. Most of the other disciples were known for some outstanding weakness, but nothing uncomplimentary is mentioned about Judas' character before meeting Jesus.

He had a good start, some excellent traits, and was considered an outstanding man. At the start of his career, he was man enough to appreciate Jesus. He felt attracted by Jesus' spell. Judas was so attracted to Jesus that he went to the lengths of attaching himself to Jesus, which implies that he was a man who had depth and feeling. Judas had higher ideals than the average man, and at one time he was a better and finer man than most.

Judas was a man of promise. Jesus recognized him as a man with high qualities, undoubtedly seeing in Judas a man of great possibilities, a man who seemed to be a natural leader. Jesus must have regarded Judas highly.

He picked Judas and the others to be His closest associates only after a long night of prayer. Obviously, Jesus felt that the Father had had a hand in the choice of The Twelve. In other words, Judas started out with the same sense of divine commission that the others had in Jesus' eyes.

We must remember that Jesus picked The Twelve from among many disciples, but He apparently felt so strongly drawn to these twelve men that He wanted them for His closest friends. It is safe to assume that Judas originally was a person worthy of trust because Jesus obviously believed in Judas. He looked on the man from Kerioth as a sincere and faithful companion.

Jesus thought enough of Judas to send him with the others on a special preaching mission. When they all returned, Jesus welcomed Judas with the others as a beloved and trusted follower. During Jesus' ministry, He consistently shared His friendship with Judas.

At first, Judas even had a good reputation among the others of The Twelve. In fact, he must have stood out as a leader among them, since they appointed him to handle their funds. They, too, trusted him and turned over their common purse to him, which seems to indicate Judas was honest and trustworthy. It also hints that he was looked up to as a careful, capable and intelligent man.

Were Judas living today (before his downfall), he would be highly respected by us. He seems to have been a model citizen. He was a stable person, he never pushed himself like James or John, and he never made rash promises or went in for big boasts like Peter. He was quiet, businesslike and respectable. Up to this point, we are not too different from Judas. It is frightening to realize that a man so like one of us can sink to such depths.

What soured Judas? How could a man with so much promise end up a traitor and a suicide? Why did Judas betray Jesus? Why? Matthew and Mark report that it was merely greed. Somehow, this does not satisfy, for if it were greed, why did Judas return the thirty pieces of silver? Furthermore, thirty pieces of silver amounted to very little. A piece of silver in those days was worth about seventy-two cents; thirty pieces gave Judas only about twenty-one dollars. This can hardly be called much of a reward for a truly greedy man.

Luke and John "explain" Judas' action by stating that "Satan entered into him," the common way of explaining anything puzzling in the first century. Anyone who behaved abnormally was believed to be possessed by demons. We readily admit that we are somewhat uncertain as to exactly what the gospel writer meant when he wrote of "Satan entering into him," but we do know, however, that Jesus healed mentally and emotionally disturbed people. If Judas were "entered" by "Satan," why did Jesus not cast out the devil? If it were simply a matter of demon-possession in Judas, we cannot help but wonder why Jesus did not have compassion on this member of The Twelve and heal him.

Human personality is too complex for anyone to say definitely why Judas betrayed Jesus. The more we study Judas, however, the more it appears he let lower ideals crowd in and master him. Judas saw the highest, but he did not let the highest rule him. He intended to give Jesus his supreme loyalty, but he let lesser loyalties push aside the supreme loyalty.

One lesser loyalty that captured Judas was the national-Messiah-loyalty. Judas was disillusioned when Jesus refused to be crowned King and conform to the popular idea of Messiah. Judas had ambition. He wanted to see his homeland free and his enemies kicked out. Judas was a patriot. He loved his country and was sure that Jesus would be the man of action to save Israel.

When Judas saw that Jesus' days were numbered and his cause was doomed, he was fed up. He decided to salvage what he could from a vain cause and get out while the getting was good.

There can be only one supreme loyalty in life: loyalty to God. All other allegiances—even allegiance to state, to church, to friends, to family—*everything* comes second to God.

Judas put himself ahead of Jesus. In the struggle between Judas and Jesus, Judas chose Judas. The inevitable deterioration of character followed, for he had taken the first step toward suicide when he put himself ahead of Jesus: "Whosoever will save his life shall lose it." Although Judas had felt the attraction of Jesus and had started out to give Him his loyalty, he had not let Jesus keep his complete allegiance. Self-destruction followed inevitably in the killing process of putting self ahead of God. Selfishness is suicide by degrees.

With Judas, the killing process continued until he at last took the final step of tying a rope around his neck, and so ended the life of a man who might have been. The fearful thing about this is that it could be any of us.

We have not looked at Judas' real mistake, however. His biggest mistake was simply this: not repenting and receiving Jesus' forgiveness on the night he betrayed the Master. Actually there was little difference between Judas and Peter that fateful night. Each sank to an unbelievable low, and each in his own way completely forsook Jesus. Yet one died and the other lived; one was lost and the other was saved. Peter repented; Judas did not.

Jesus certainly gave Judas every opportunity. Even as Judas led the mob to arrest Jesus, Jesus greeted Judas with a manner and words that carried hope and friendship. In fact, the very term that Jesus used to greet Judas was the word "Friend." "Friend" may sound a bit stiff and formal in English, but in its original form it was a term of greeting between close acquaintances. We could roughly translate it as "Buddy" or "Pal."

Jesus held out every offer of forgiveness to Judas, but Judas refused to be forgiven. God cannot make us accept forgiveness. The choice is ours: we can accept; or we can refuse. Judas refused, and so died the most tragic figure in human history.

The incident shows the greatness of the love that was in Jesus. It must have been heartbreaking for Him when one of the trusted Twelve turned traitor, *but Jesus could even forgive Judas!* We have not begun to guess how big is the heart of God!

So, even from the tragic mess of Judas' life, we can learn how great is God's forgiveness. If Jesus could forgive Judas, He can even forgive you or me. What more can anyone ask!